BRAIN TWISTERS FOR
MINECRAFTERS

PUZZLES AND HEADSCRATCHERS FOR OVERWORLD FUN

BRAIN TWISTERS FOR MINECRAFTERS

PUZZLES AND HEADSCRATCHERS FOR OVERWORLD FUN

BRIAN BOONE

Illustrations by Amanda Brack

Sky Pony Press
New York

BRAIN TWISTERS FOR MINECRAFTERS.

Copyright © 2020 by Hollan Publishing, Inc.

Minecraft® is a registered trademark of Notch Development AB. The *Minecraft* game is copyright © Mojang AB.

Sky Pony Press books may be purchased in bulk at special discounts for sales promotion, corporate gifts, fund-raising, or educational purposes. Special editions can also be created to specifications. For details, contact the Special Sales Department, Sky Pony Press, 307 West 36th Street, 11th Floor, New York, NY 10018 or info@skyhorsepublishing.com.

Sky Pony® is a registered trademark of Skyhorse Publishing, Inc.®, a Delaware corporation.

Visit our website at www.skyponypress.com.

10 9 8 7 6 5 4 3 2 1

Library of Congress Cataloging-in-Publication Data is available on file.

Cover illustration by Amanda Brack
Cover design by Brian Peterson

Paperback ISBN: 978-1-5107-4729-6
E-book ISBN: 978-1-5107-4740-1

Printed in the United States of America

TABLE OF CONTENTS

INTRODUCTION

Attention all Minecrafters! Don't be alarmed, but we're
about to blow your mind like a creeper holding a TNT
block. But unlike that green goblin, we don't want to break
anything. We just want to dust off the cobwebs, stretch your
mind muscles, and get you thinking to solve a huge lode of
Minecraft puzzles. Grab your (logical) pickaxe and (mental)
sword, and dig into *Brain Twisters for Minecrafters*.

The first brain twister to unravel: What is a "brain twister?"
A brain twister is a clever little question for you to figure out
the answer to — a little bit of a word problem and a little bit
of a joke. Brain twisters are riddles to the extreme, as each
one is a fun little test for your mind. Pay close attention to
every word, remember what you know about *Minecraft* (a
lot!), and give them your best shot. You'll feel smart when
you crack them, and they'll make you laugh too.

Brain Twisters for Minecrafters is the ultimate *Minecraft*
game (besides *Minecraft* itself, of course). In these pages
you'll find all kinds of fun brain games about mobs, biomes,
Steve, Alex, tools, and ores galore. Let's get in there and
pick your brain, Minecrafter!

CHAPTER 1: MINE TWISTERS FROM MANY MOBS

Alex has bred seventeen sheep. But then a hostile mob runs through and kills all but nine of them. How many sheep does Alex have left?

Nine. (It was a trick question.)

Where do creepers go after an explosion?

They go everywhere!

Steve comes across a Jack o' Lantern and a couple of sticks in the middle of a grassy biome. What's the meaning of this?

It was a snow golem . . . but it melted. Its carved pumpkin head and stick arms are all that's left of it.

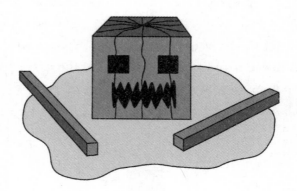

This mob isn't smart enough to do math, so it can't add or subtract. But it's definitely been known to multiply. What is it?

A rabbit.

■

A creeper is after Steve, so he has to find safety in one of three structures. One is on fire, one is full of skeletons, and the other is home to spiders who haven't eaten in months. Which place is the safest?

The structure with the spiders. If they haven't eaten in months, those spiders are very much dead.

If skeletons always shoot Steve in the knees, where would they shoot kid Steve?

In his kid-knees.

■

If ghasts had feet, what would they wear on them?

Boo-ts.

What are a wither skeleton, a skeleton, and redstone?

Black and white and red all over.

■

What's the difference between a creeper and a balloon?

One blows itself up, while the other you have to blow up yourself.

■

What do you call a zombie pigman that steals your sword?

A HAMburglar.

What do you call a zombie with no eyes?

A zombe.

■

How do you make a witch scratch?

Take away the w from "witch" and you get itch . . . that needs to get scratched.

■

Alex is in the Taiga Biome with a pack on her back, but she isn't carrying anything. How is this possible?

The pack is a pack of wolves, and they're on her back, which means they're chasing her.

You could call me a sow, but don't call me a cow. I like to plow and you could spawn me now. What am I?

A pig.

Build this type of room into your structure if you want to avoid zombies, because you're not likely to find them there. What room is it?

A living room.

■

I build structures for homes all the time, yet I never use a block. What am I?

A spider. (They spin their own webs from their string.)

■

What in *Minecraft* is actually and clearly made up of liquid, yet could die if it gets wet?

Slime.

■

What can make color, but can never change its own color?

A squid. (It makes ink.)

■

I may be harmless, but I am certainly not defenseless. (Let's just stay away from each other.) What am I?

A pigman.

■

It's ruthless and rare, and it sounds like it might sit on the top of your head. What is it?

A killer bunny. (A bunny might be called a hare, which sounds like "hair," which sits on top of your head.)

Who ride horses in the real world, but not in *Minecraft*?

Jockeys.

■

We've got nobody, but we've got each other. And there are plenty of us. What are we?

Skeletons.

■

Goldfish don't seem to get much older, but how can you make one suddenly age?

Remove the "g" from goldfish, and you've got an "oldfish."

■

When is a "might" a definite?

When it's an endermite.

■

Three mobs are in a boat and it capsizes. None of them gets wet, although they all go under. Why?

The mobs are witches, and it's merely their hats that got wet.

■

What's dead but alive, and if there's one of them, there's always two more in tow?

A witch.

This mob only wants a part of you, as it has no use for all of you. Which mob is it?

A zombie.

What's the difference between a fly and a vex?

A vex can fly, but a fly can't vex.

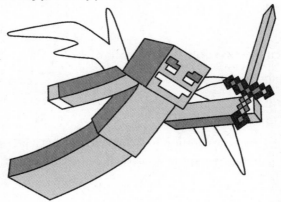

This mob has no arms, yet it is very armed. What is it?

A creeper. (They don't have arms, but they're "armed" in that they can explode at any time.)

What lives among the living but does not actually live?

A zombie.

What can make a big and powerful splash without going anywhere near the water?

Witches.

We're fond of huts, but you'll never see us on the football field. What are we?

Witches.

■

What can fly through walls, but isn't a ghast?

A vex.

■

What's more invisible than the phantom?

The phantom's shadow.

■

We didn't give the solution to this brain twister a lot of ink in this book, but this thing never lacks for ink. What is it?

A squid.

■

What has a skull, but is not a skeleton?

A Wither.

■

What's green and has no arms, but isn't a creeper?

Slime.

■

Why can't a creeper clap?

Because it has no hands.

What's the only way an ocelot could change its spots?

By moving from one spot to another!

■

If all of the *Minecraft* cows talked at once, what would they say?

Not much, seeing as how cows can't talk.

■

What color socks do polar bears wear?

They don't wear socks—they have bear feet.

■

Don't grumble at my mumbles, my message remains clear. (Boo!) What am I?

A ghast.

■

What are black or white and found all over?

Sheep.

■

What rattles but would frighten a baby?

A skeleton.

■

What can make you hungry while also making you ill?

A husk.

What will gladly attack you, but run away if you try to attack it?

An evoker.

◾

What evokes but isn't an evoker?

A vex.

◾

How can a hostile mob be a building block?

When it's slime.

◾

What is hostile and comes in threes? (It's not a witch.)

A Wither. (It's got three heads.)

◾

What do a creeper and a Wither have in common?

The suffix "-er."

◾

Why does the Ender Dragon have a hard time understanding books?

Because it always starts at The End.

◾

Among all the heavy ores and stones, how is it that bones could be the heaviest items in all of *Minecraft*?

*Because bones are what make up skele-*tons.

Whose job in *Minecraft* is it to get fired?

A blaze.

■

What dies as it lives?

Sheep. (Or rather, it can dye *its wool and keep on living, no problem.)*

■

What kind of horse in *Minecraft* has six legs?

One that's being ridden by Steve or Alex.

■

How many *Minecraft* horses have three legs?

All of them have three legs (at least).

■

Why do white sheep eat more than black sheep?

There are more of them in the Overworld, so of course they eat more.

■

How do you spell "endermite" backward?

E-N-D-E-R-M-I-T-E B-A-C-K-W-A-R-D.

■

What in *Minecraft* has six eyes and twelve legs?

A trio of witches.

BRAIN TWISTERS FOR MINECRAFTERS

Think carefully here. How many sides does a slime cube have?

It's not six—it's twelve. Look closely and you'll see that a slime cube is a cube inside another cube. That means there are six sides on the outside cube and another six on the inside cube, which makes twelve in all.

■

All it needs is a name, and it can give me any color of clothing I could ever want.

A sheep . . . if you name it "jeb_."

■

What has bones but not flesh, and has a face but not skin?

A skeleton.

■

What can hang out in the sun all day but not be affected by the sun's heat in any way?

A husk.

■

What animal can sow but not plow?

A pig.

■

I am known to be harmless, yet I am not defenseless. (Just covering my bases.) What am I?

A pigman.

When I'm not lurking around *Minecraft*, I'm a private investigator and a government agent, too. What am I?

A P.I. g-man.

■

I fly high in the Nether, and I share a fearsome foe with you. Who am I?

The Wither. (It fears the Ender Dragon, too.)

■

What wears a coat in the winter and pants in the summer?

A dog.

■

What two words can immediately summon both a horse and a sheep?

"Hay, ewe!"

■

What kind of fireman doesn't put out fires?

A blaze.

■

Imagine you're in a boat in the middle of the ocean. Suddenly, you're surrounded by angry elder guardians. How can you put an end to this and go somewhere safe?

Hit "restart" on your Minecraft *game.*

How can you have a skeleton on the outside and still be alive?

When you're a spider with a skeleton on your back.

■

It's one of a crowd and sits there, undisturbed, like a needle in a haystack. What is it?

Monster egg.

■

They guard a treasure, not knowing what that treasure is. What are they?

Guardians.

■

At the beginning of the game, you seek me out. I clothe you and can feed you, too. What am I?

Sheep.

■

Many things can explode in *Minecraft*. What is the only explosive thing that can move and blow up without being lit?

A creeper.

■

They roam while others sleep, looking for food that's hiding from them. What are they?

Zombies.

I look cute and cuddly, but don't cross me or you're done for, and that's the cold truth. What am I?

A polar bear.

What's a shell of its former self, and is far more dangerous in that form?

A shulker.

What stays where it is when it goes off?

A creeper.

Why do skeletons move around alone?

Ah, because they've got no body.

Where is there cowhide in *Minecraft*?

It covers all the cows.

■

What's cute and cuddly and fuzzy and deadly?

The killer bunny.

■

What creature is as graceful as it is hideous, and as harmless?

The squid.

■

What time is it when a creeper blows up your house?

Time to get a new house.

■

Unlike most living things, if you give this one warmth, it will probably die. But keep it supremely cold, and it'll live on. What is it?

A snow golem.

■

Which side of an ocelot has the most fur?

The outside.

I'd never be rude to you, and I wave my tongue like a flag for all to see. What am I?

A dog.

■

I can be every color of the rainbow, if you know what to say. What am I?

I'm a sheep that's been named jeb_.

■

What is the smallest yet largest mob in *Minecraft*?

The slime cube.

■

I'm supposed to kill you and move you away from your spot, but my actions wind up taking my life even if I don't successfully claim yours. What am I?

A creeper.

■

Could an Ender Dragon lift Steve with just one hand?

No, because Ender Dragons don't have hands.

■

Creepers can easily destroy structures and players, so how do you get one to destroy itself?

Give it a mirror.

You can see right through me, yet you still fear me. What am I?

A skeleton.

It most likely smells very bad when it's alive, but quite good just after it's dead. What is it?

A pig. It doesn't smell great on a farm, but when a player makes cooked pork, it likely smells great.

What is taller when it sits down than when it stands?

A dog.

They're sworn enemies, but what do a creeper and an ocelot actually have in common?

The letter "c."

Who's someone who brings things to a close—er, *maybe* they do?

End-er-mite. (They "end" but also, "er," they might or "mite" not.)

Listen carefully, because just before it explodes, a creeper breaks something. They do it every time. What is it?

They break the silence.

On what day might you find pigs and various pigmen rolling around in the dirt?

On "Ground Hog" Day.

■

Shulkers aren't just called "shulkers." They have names like you and me. What's the most common name for a shulker?

Shelly.

■

If a guardian had a name, what would it be?

Spike.

■

What's the best name you could give a husk?

Sunny.

■

If a zombie pigman were a food, what kind of food would it be?

Back bacon.

■

To whom would you say hello, hello, hello?

A Wither.

■

What burns in the daytime, unless it's in the shade?

A zombie.

Which is the smartest of the hostile mobs?

The Wither, because it has three heads, and three heads are better than one.

What do you call a zombie pigman that has three eyes?

A zombie piiigman.

What makes up a trio of witches?

The third witch does.

You know that creepers don't have hands, but what in *Minecraft* has just one hand?

An arm.

What do you call a pig that stands in the sun for too long?

Bacon!

Spelling test time. Can you spell "mob" with three letters, but without using the letters "m" or "b"?

F-O-E.

■

What part of a chicken has the most feathers?

The outside of the chicken.

■

Of all the neutral and tamable mobs in *Minecraft*, which ones would make the best neighbors?

The horses, because they say "neigh" all the time.

■

What do you call a silverfish that doesn't have any eyes?

A slverfsh.

■

What sleeps at day and flies at night without the aid of feathers or propulsion from a human player in any way?

A bat.

■

What is there a lot of in *Minecraft*, even if there is just one?

An oce-lot.

What scary thing would you call a horse wandering the Overland at night?

A night-mare.

◼

How do you spawn a puddle from a hostile mob in a hot biome like the desert?

Send a snow golem there.

◼

If your tamed wolf wanders into a hot biome and gets uncomfortable, what should you give her?

Mustard. It's great on hot dogs!

◼

What do *Minecraft* cows have that no other animals in *Minecraft* have?

Baby cows.

This may be a hostile mob, but it's certainly the most valuable of all mobs. What is it?

The silverfish.

■

Two creepers were walking outside the village one day. The first suggested they go left, but the other wanted to go right. They wound up going left, where they got chased for an hour by an ocelot. When they finally lost the cat, the creeper who had wanted to go right was furious with the first creeper, who'd insisted on going left. What did she say to him?

She said, "ssssssssss," because that's all creepers can say.

■

Is it possible to lift a creeper with just one hand?

Probably not, because there's no such thing as a creeper with just one hand.

■

How do you make a *Minecraft* dog into a Scotty dog (without using any special mods)?

Get into its details and rename it Scotty!

■

While there are no locks on doors or windows in *Minecraft*, this neutral mob does come pretty close to doing the job. What is it?

Salmon. (Another name for salmon is lox.)

It's one of the scariest mobs in *Minecraft*, although they've never hurt you or any other player you've heard about. What is it?

Ocelots. They're quite scary...to creepers.

■

Which of the passive mobs is also the most ticklish in all of *Minecraft*?

Squids. After all, their bodies are covered in ten-tickles.

■

How are the pigs and horses in *Minecraft* similar to one another?

When pigs are hungry, they'll eat like a horse, and when horses are hungry, they'll eat like pigs.

■

Why are pigs a terrible mob to reveal secrets to?

Because they will often squeal.

■

How do you make a creeper smile?

Turn it upside down.

CHAPTER 2: CRAFTING ABOUT AND TOOLING AROUND

There is just one thing you can put in a stone to make it lighter. And it works on every single kind of stone, rock, and ore in *Minecraft*. What is it?

A hole.

■

You might love *Minecraft* and think it's pretty exciting. Can you name the one time when the game is extremely boring?

When you're drilling holes.

■

This *Minecraft* tool is all-encompassing, yet it does just one thing. What is it?

*A compass. (It's all-*encompassing, *get it?)*

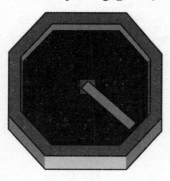

What item in *Minecraft* is black when you mine it, orange when you use it, and grey when it's all used up?

Coal.

■

Why are kid Minecrafters so good at finding ore?

Because they're "minors."

■

A pickaxe can be used to break through, break into, or break down many different substances in *Minecraft*. What's the one thing Steve could "pick" with his axe that would hurt him?

His nose.

■

This material is absolutely everywhere in *Minecraft*. Despite that abundance, you probably never notice it, or if you do, you get rid of it. What is it?

Dirt!

■

There hasn't been a *Minecraft* update yet in which the programmers added dinosaurs. (Too bad!) However, there is the occasional dino. How is that possible?

There's dino-mite in Minecraft. Or rather dynamite, *another word for "TNT."*

It doesn't matter how spectacular a playing session you have, what you build, or what mobs you face; this is guaranteed to be the highlight of almost every *Minecraft* game. What is it?

A torch. They're mounted on walls, so one is truly a "high light."

■

Yes, I'm very sharp. And yes, I do have a point. I'm not Steve or Alex or Notch. What am I?

I'm a sword.

■

No matter if you have Steve run around in his usual shirt and pants or put him in some fancy armor, this choice will always look sharp. What is it?

A pickaxe or sword. They're always sharp. (We didn't say they had to be clothing options.)

■

I'm not human or a mob. I don't really have many physical features at all. But if you're feeling it, you just might say I'm a hunk. What am I?

A slab. ("Hunk" and "slab" mean the same thing.)

■

If you punch this, it'll give you a hard time . . . but no hard feelings. What is it?

A tree. The "hard time" it will give you is wood, and it won't give you "hard feelings" because it's just a tree.

I'm a ruler, but I don't lord over a kingdom, only an individual. But where I'm at could mean the difference between life and death . . . for you. What am I?

A health meter.

What's always running but isn't an animal, hostile mob, or player?

A clock.

What's the easiest way to make a lighthouse in *Minecraft*?

Put a torch in a building. Boom! You just made a light-house.

What in *Minecraft* works better, not worse, when it's tired?

A mine cart. They need tires to roll, don't they?

What's the most sought-after thing in *Minecraft* with absolutely no value or special use?

A dragon egg.

By themselves, they're basically useless. But put them together and they make a great team. Goodness, their names even rhyme! What are they?

A bow and arrow.

What's the difference between the law and an ice block?

One is justice . . . and the other is just ice.

■

This will show you where you're going. You don't need to ask it a question, and it won't utter a word. What is it?

A map.

■

What do you have to pick before *it* can pick?

A pickaxe.

■

What has branches and roots but no family?

A tree.

■

This explodes, but it isn't a creeper. It doesn't blow up anything except for itself. It's found and mined. So what is it?

Obsidian.

■

You can build this, but it just might destroy you in the end. What is it?

TNT.

What may go out even when if it stays put?

A torch.

■

What has four legs but never runs?

A chair.

■

The more you take from me, the bigger I get. What am I?

A hole.

■

What has cities, towns, and streets, but no people?

A map.

■

In *Minecraft*, there is a coat. No matter what you do it (or don't do to it), it will always be wet. What kind of coat is it?

A coat of paint.

■

What element in *Minecraft* can be used to live in while living but could also be used to live in during death?

Wood. It can be used to build a house . . . or a coffin.

It makes a cart go, but if you rearrange the letters it becomes more familiar. What is it?

An axle. Switch those letters around and it becomes Alex.

■

For what item in *Minecraft* could you write an autobiography?

A mine cart. It's the closest thing to a car, also called an "automobile."

■

Sometimes I'm green, sometimes I'm yellow. But I'm never red. What am I?

An experience orb.

■

I contain an infinite number of items bigger and heavier than I am. Even after you destroy me, I don't let go of my stock. What am I?

A shulker box.

■

There are lots of coats of armor in *Minecraft*. What kind of coat has no sleeves, no pockets in which to put things, and won't keep you warm . . . or even safe?

It's not a coat of armor—it's a coat of paint that goes on the inside or outside of a building.

What imposing thing in *Minecraft* is tall, green, and not something you want to hug? (It's not what you think it is.)

A cactus. (See? It wasn't a creeper!)

■

What has two legs, and can lean, but doesn't ever walk?

A ladder.

■

What can you do to a wall that will allow you to walk through it?

Install a door in that wall, and you can pass right through it.

■

For hours, Steve mined in a place where he heard both diamonds and emeralds were plentiful. At the end of the day, what did he get?

Tired.

■

What goes in a house and goes up and down while remaining fixed in place?

Stairs.

■

What living thing has a bark but isn't a dog?

A tree.

I brighten your day while staying in the shade. What am I?

A torch.

■

What has a head and body and flies with feathers . . . but how far it goes depends on you?

An arrow.

■

You might describe me as being extremely sharp, yet I don't actually have a brain. What am I?

A pickaxe.

■

It's a blade, but it won't cut you if you touch it. All it can really cut through is the wind. What is it?

A blade of grass.

■

How do you fix a redstone short circuit?

Make it longer.

■

What has dozens of limbs but can't walk or hug?

A tree.

■

What must rise before it can fall?

A pickaxe.

What can hold more than its own size in treasures and finds?

A chest.

■

What comes with a bow but isn't a present?

Arrows.

What's full of ticks but isn't a dog, a wolf, or any other kind of animal?

A clock.

■

What ore can you mine with a tool made out of itself?

Gold ore.

■

If you can't see in the sea, I can help you see in the sea, if you can see enough in the sea to see me. What am I?

A sea lantern.

■

I am a block, but you can't hold me, place me, or mine me, or see me. What am I?

An air block.

What odd *Minecraft* substance is technically as hard as a rock but softer than dirt?

Netherrack.

■

What has rings but no fingers?

A tree.

■

What does a good job only after it's fired?

Fireworks rockets.

■

When is a block made of nothing?

When it's an air block.

■

What is useful when you start but painful when you're done?

Glass, used for making window panes (pains).

■

You can fight or hunt with words, so long as you rearrange them first. How?

A sword. Move the "s" on "words" to the front of "word," and you get "sword"!

Two of Steve's most useful weapons and tools are always at his side, even if he isn't carrying anything. What are they?

His fists.

What can you cast aside and always have it return to you?

A fishing line.

What is black and blue but never at the same time?

Obsidian.

You're holding me right now, and I'm never seen without my companion. What am I?

A book (with a quill).

■

We often work as a team. Destroy our base, we die. Destroy our colony, the base lives. What are we?

Trees.

■

Water disappears when I am near. What am I?

A sponge.

■

You can create almost anything in *Minecraft*, but this is the one thing that limits what you can do. If not for this, things could stretch into the skies and stars and it would be complete and total chaos. What is it?

The building height restriction barrier.

■

This could come in handy. It only points in the direction from which you came, but also points to the way home. It could be the most treasured and useful tool in your arsenal. What is it?

A compass.

Is there an afterlife in *Minecraft*? Who knows, but there's this kind of dirt. What is it?

Soul sand.

◼

It begins in the beginning yet knows how to delay the end, and while its powers are potentially endless, it can help just one individual. What is it?

A Nether star (which can be used to make beacons).

◼

It glows with mystery, but you can't get to it without defeating a good defense. What is it?

A well-guarded prismarine lamp.

◼

What's something in *Minecraft* that players will do anything for even though it won't do anything for those players?

A dragon egg.

◼

Steve came across a tiny grove of just three trees. He did to the first tree what he did to the third tree, and did to the second tree what he did to the third tree. What happened to each tree if the second tree got punched down?

Steve punched all of them down.

What kind of bench wouldn't you sit on?

A work bench.

■

What doesn't work, but once worked under pressure?

A diamond.

■

What doesn't have wings but flies, and has no teeth and still bites?

A fired arrow.

■

It goes on a gift or can send pain. What is it?

A bow.

■

What do a clock and a creeper have in common?

They're both unarmed.

■

What in *Minecraft* loses its head in the morning, but gets it back at nightfall?

Steve's pillow.

■

What is brown and dirty?

Dirt.

What is the only thing that can be made from fire instead of destroyed by it?

A sword.

When are raindrops not made of water?

When it's a rain of arrows.

What *Minecraft* tool can you use to hoe a row, slay a foe, and wring with woe?

Your hands.

Can you get mail in *Minecraft*?

You can if it's chainmail.

What tool can be used to greet, and can also be used to describe the tallest structure you ever built?

The word "hi" (high).

You're in a mine cart and you see three structures. One has a gold door, one has a quartz door, and one has a wooden door. Which door do you open first?

The cart door.

It blooms only when provoked, yet it's not a flower. It can help you live, or help you die. What is it?

It's fire.

■

When purple is born, I die. What am I?

Lava.

■

What's infinite in *Minecraft* and right under your feet the whole time?

Dirt.

■

Steve has nothing in his inventory but a stone axe, eight wooden planks, and four sticks. Okay, so he has *one* more item in his inventory. What is it?

It's a pickaxe. He must have had one to craft a stone axe without cobblestone.

■

I am not a bird but I have feathers and I fly. What am I?

An arrow.

■

Carry me with you, but place me in a specific location and I will hurt you. What am I?

A lava bucket.

It's not a mob or player, but it provides information without speaking and you can understand what it says. What is it?

A sign.

■

I'm the most useless item, but some might call me the most effective weapon. What am I?

A dead bush.

■

What kind of crystals don't break when they hit the ground?

Ice and snow crystals.

■

What's the dirtiest word you can think of in *Minecraft*?

"Dirt."

■

What's the name of the boat inside *Minecraft*?

Raft—it's inside Minecraft.

■

How can Alex make a table bigger by using something that comes from a tree that isn't wood?

She could use a leaf.

If Steve's special fishing tool had a name, what it would it be?

Rod.

If H₂O is the formula for water, then what's the formula for ice in *Minecraft*?

H₂O cubed.

How are the diamonds Steve mined like Steve's heart?

Both are stored in a chest.

What entity in *Minecraft* does not and cannot experience pain, but can still live a painful existence?

A house with lots of windows. Window glass is made from "panes," so in other words, it's "pane-ful" (painful).

■

What tool is almost completely see-through?

Shears (sheers).

■

What roars but doesn't have a mouth from which it can scream?

An explosion.

■

You'd find this on top of a present, or in the hands of a hostile mob pointing it at you. What is it?

A bow.

You can't mine this in *Minecraft*. You can't see it. But if you eat it, you'll die.

Nothing!

■

While Alex was working at her crafting table, she took the clock off the wall and put it under that crafting table. Why?

She needed to work over time.

■

How many bricks does it take to complete a tower made entirely of bricks?

One, as the last one completes the tower.

■

When did Steve feel swell when he also felt bad?

When he accidentally hit his hand with a shovel.

■

I am inside Steve but you can see it on the screen. What is it?

Hearts.

■

I may be full of holes, but I can still hold plenty of water. What am I?

A sponge.

You'll never find me on a map, but you'll find a map on me. What am I?

Paper.

■

What common find in *Minecraft* has a neck but no head?

A glass bottle.

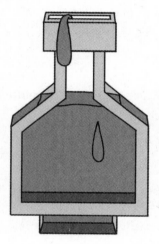

What can you drop from a tall building and it will land safely and survive, but if you drop it in water, it will shrivel up and die?

Paper.

■

What's the easiest way to make a chainmail helmet last?

Make the chest plate first . . . then make the chainmail helmet last.

It provides directions to others but doesn't give any to itself, even though it knows. It can tell you how to get around, and without it you'd surely get lost. What is it?

A sign.

■

What goes up and down the stairs without ever moving?

Carpet.

■

Stick your fingers in my eyes, I'll open my mouth wide. I don't even mind! What am I?

Shears.

■

You have to use me to get from space to space. Yet I always remain firmly in place. What am I?

A doorknob.

■

What's the hardest thing in a game of *Minecraft*?

The rocks and stones. They're very hard!

■

This is one of the few pets you can have in *Minecraft*, except we aren't sure you'd want to. They just lie there and don't do anything. What are they?

*Car*pets.

I've got the music in me, but I don't have a mouth to sing with, nor do I have hands to play an instrument. But still I'll make a joyful noise. What am I?

A note block.

■

What a fireplace provides can be found inside of a common crop. What is it?

Heat and wheat. ("Heat" can be found inside of the word "wheat.")

■

How many pieces of string would it take to stretch from the End to the outer reaches of the Far Lands?

Just one piece . . . if it was a long enough piece of string, that is.

■

What can you use in *Minecraft* that will allow you to look completely through a wall? (And it's not a mod.)

A window!

■

If you walk on these while they're alive, they don't make a sound. But walk on them when they're dead, they'll make a big racket about it. What are they?

Leaves. Only after they fall off a tree and die do they get crinkly and cracked and noisy to the touch.

I can fly through the air all day, but also remain standing, and also stay in just one place, right where you left me. What am I?

A banner.

∎

What would you call tiny little windows in a place where you keep treasure?

Chest panes.

∎

What ore in *Minecraft* could be used to color a sheep?

A dye-mond.

∎

It reaches for the sky, but never quite gets there. So instead, it just stays on the ground, hanging around and barking. What is it?

It's a tree. It grows tall to "reach for the sky," so it hangs around "barking," meaning it's covered in bark.

∎

What can you use to make slaw or a torch?

Coal (or cole).

∎

What can totally cover certain hills, and also bite even though it lacks a mouth, teeth, or even a face?

Frost.

I may be hard and stony, but I'm not made of ore or metal. If you take me to the wrong place, I'll disappear forever. What am I?

I am ice. (It's hard like stone and if you take it to a warm biome, it will melt.)

■

This is a stone made for sleeping, but you can't sleep on it, nor can you make a bed out of it. You can't even get *rid* of it. What is it?

Bedrock.

■

What can a sheep step on that won't kill it, but will, in a way, make it die?

A flower. (It dyes *the sheep's wool a different color.)*

A pickaxe tried to tell a riddle to a tree, but it couldn't guess it. Why was that?

It was stumped.

What can you add to a bucket that holds milk or lava to make it hold less milk or lava?

A hole.

■

This can be made of stone, brick, quartz, or wood. What in the Overworld is it?

A slab.

■

Alex recently built a grand temple out of a huge variety of resources. Steve already had two temples, however, and he didn't use a single piece of wood or stone. How is that possible?

He has a temple on each side of his head.

■

I'm actually just a loosely connected collection of holes. I'm strong as metal but also quite flexible. What am I?

I am chainmail armor.

■

What happened to Steve that caused him to be mad and simultaneously delighted?

Alex stole all of his torches. That made him mad, not to mention de-lighted, as in he had no more light.

Think about your arsenal of *Minecraft* tools and weapons. What can you use to 1) dig for ore, 2) fight mobs, and 3) mine metallic blocks?

1) A shovel, 2) a sword, and 3) a pickaxe. We didn't say the answer had to be just one *thing.*

CHAPTER 3: CONFOODING FUSE ZUPPLES, OR RATHER CONFUSING FOOD PUZZLES

When is the best time for Steve or Alex to eat?

Whenever they're hungry.

■

Raw beef is a well-known food item in *Minecraft*. So how do you make ground beef in the game?

Make a cow lie down. A cow on the ground=ground beef.

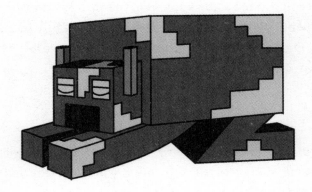

What in *Minecraft* sounds like a parrot but isn't a mob, hostile or otherwise?

A carrot.

Gold has many uses in *Minecraft*. How can you make a gold soup in the game without using any ore whatsoever?

You use fourteen carrots (karats).

■

You'll only see this when it dies. But it's pretty tasty, cooked and fried. What is it?

Fish.

■

Minecraft is a little different from the real world. In what situation would you stop on green but go on red?

When you're eating a watermelon slice—you don't eat the green part, but you do eat the red part.

■

Steve harvested some apples on Tuesday and ate a third of them that day. The next day, he ate half of what was left. On day three, he saw only two apples were left. How many did he originally harvest?

Six.

■

Think of an egg in *Minecraft*. Which of these statements about it is correct: "the egg yolk is white" or "the yolk of the egg is white"?

Neither is correct, because egg yolks are yellow, not white.

Out of what common flower in *Minecraft* could you craft a soda?

A poppy.

◼

Say you've got half of a potato. What object in *Minecraft* looks exactly like that half of a potato?

The other half of a potato.

◼

Did you know that whenever Steve or Alex eats a food creation in *Minecraft*, they also eat over an inch of dirt? How is that possible? Why would they do that?

Because no matter where they eat, they're eating over the ground, or "an inch of dirt." If they sit or stand, the dirt-covered ground is always underneath them.

Not a single piece of armor, potion, weapon, enchantment, or anything else can stop me. Well, a potato or an apple could. What am I?

I'm hunger.

■

I'm hungry and need to get full. Fill me up with milk or lava; either is fine. What am I?

A bucket.

■

They're not on the regular list of food items you can grow, so how do you grow strawberries in *Minecraft*?

Plant blocks of hay . . . then you'll get "straw" berries.

■

I'm presently a tasty fish, but I used to be quite odorous. What am I?

Smelt.

■

What common room can you not build in *Minecraft*?

A mushroom!

■

How can a tree catch food?

When you use a tree's wood to make a fishing rod.

This may have lots of eyes, yet it cannot see a thing. What is it?

A potato.

∎

What contains ore but cannot be mined?

An orange.

What was once fruit but now glows?

A Jack o'Lantern.

How can you make lemons in *Minecraft*?

Rearrange the letters in "MELONS."

∎

What is brown and found underground, but isn't dirt?

Potatoes.

∎

What kind of room in *Minecraft* can only be brown or red?

A mushroom.

What helps you live by not living?

Animals—you can eat them.

■

How do you make a hot biome into something you'd want to eat?

Add an "s" to Desert and you get dessert.

■

Some call me by the name of the creator, and I can make you nearly invincible. What am I?

A Notch apple.

■

It helps others to grow so those things will in turn grow others. It comes from an end to bring about something new. Neat! What is it?

It's bone meal.

■

What can Alex fight with a potato that a weapon won't touch?

Hunger.

■

How many apples grow on a tree in *Minecraft*?

All the apples in Minecraft grow on one tree or another.

How many ounces of milk can you put in an empty bucket?

Just a few drops. Once there's any lava in that bucket, it's no longer an "empty bucket."

■

I do exist, but not in the material world. I'm made of numbers, but I'm also square. I build amongst my own kind, and can make anything, and sometimes I stand perfectly still and don't do anything . . . which proves incredibly useful. What am I?

Minecraft blocks.

■

What kind of seed doesn't ever grow up to become a plant or food?

A world seed.

■

I'm red here in *Minecraft*, but to you I might also be green or yellow. What am I?

An apple.

■

What vegetable might you find in a note block?

Beets.

I'm a well-known meal, yet I cannot be eaten by your player. What am I?

Bone meal.

■

How do you make an apple tart in *Minecraft*?

Take a single apple and dip it into a sour-tasting potion.

■

Even though it's not one of the "official" foods, did you know you can make a squash in *Minecraft*? How would you go about doing that?

Take a pumpkin, throw it in the air, and wait for it to "squash" onto the ground below. (Fun fact: A pumpkin is itself a type of squash.)

This is an old one, and people have tried to find an answer for centuries. So, which came first: the chicken or the egg? In *Minecraft*, there's an answer.

In Minecraft, *the chickens come first. You don't see eggs until you raise chickens, and you might never see a dragon egg!*

If you could make a fish in *Minecraft*, what would it be?

Smelt.

■

What would you get if you fed a bunch of diamonds to a cow?

Blue cheese.

■

Using only a sword, how many slices can you cut from a brand-new whole slab of beef?

Just one slice. After you cut a slice, it's no longer a whole slab of beef.

It's a thing you drink but it's also a thing that Steve does. What is it?

Punch.

■

What does Alex never eat for breakfast?

Lunch and dinner.

■

If you took two apples from three apples, how many apples would you have?

Two apples – you only took the two.

■

Every day, Steve takes his stew and bread and stands over a mineshaft while he eats. Why does he do this?

He wants to eat foods that are "holesome" (wholesome).

■

What's the easiest food to eat in *Minecraft*?

A piece of cake.

■

When making food, what's the very best thing to put into a stew?

Your spoon.

Milk is a food, and it can go sour and make Steve and Alex quite sick. What's the best way to prevent that milk from spoiling?

Just leave it in the cow.

■

What's about the only thing that's more useful if it's broken?

An egg.

■

It doesn't eat food, but it does enjoy a light meal. What is it?

Plants and flowers. They stay alive with photosynthesis, which is how plants make food out of light.

■

What drops from a very, very, *very* bad chicken?

Deviled eggs.

■

What can you use to make music in *Minecraft* that isn't a note block?

A chicken. After all, it's got two drumsticks.

■

Can you name two things in *Minecraft* that contain milk?

Two cows!

What crop is musical, in that it will help you keep rhythm, and it can also help you recognize where you came from?

Beetroot. It keeps the "beet" (beat) and keeps alive your "roots."

■

There are a few trees in Alex's garden. On one of them, an apple tree, there are two apples. But then a strong wind blew through, and there were apples on neither the tree nor the ground. How's that possible?

Before the winds, there were two apples on the tree. The wind blew one to the ground, leaving one in the tree and one on the ground. That meant there weren't apples—plural—on either the tree or the ground, just a single one in each place.

■

While you can trick this thing into biting, you're the one that will bite it . . . and eat it! What is it?

Fish. You use a fishing rod to get it to "bite."

■

Think of a crop you can grow in *Minecraft*. It's five letters long. Remove the first letter and it's a word for something that provides warmth. Take away the next letter and it's something you have to do to live. What's the original word?

Wheat, which becomes "heat," which becomes "eat."

Other than getting a drop from a deceased pig, what's another way to make a pork chop in *Minecraft*?

Use karate chop on a pigman, and then you've got a pork chop.

You need to "pick" this. "Picking" this will get you far in *Minecraft*. In fact, if you "pick" this, you'll live a little longer. What is it?

An apple. (Did you think we were going to say "pickaxe?")

■

What's the only edible table you can make in *Minecraft*?

A vege-table.

■

Look at your average run-of-the-mill *Minecraft* potato. How many sides does it have?

Two—the inside and the outside.

How do you make a beetroot shake?

Give it a good scare!

What food could you grow to equal the value of just one block of gold?

Fourteen carrots.

What's the easiest and best way for Steve to raise chorus fruit?

With his hand, to his mouth.

What's the last thing Alex should put in a cake?

Her teeth!

How did Steve get fat in just a few minutes?

He cooked up a bunch of pork chops . . . which left him with quite a bit of fat left over.

■

It may seem normal to you, but what's the strangest food you can have in *Minecraft*?

A kooky (cookie).

■

Alex wanted some cooked food, but she was too tired to cook it herself. But she wound up with a nice hot meal. How did she do that?

She got someone else to cook it. (Thanks, Steve.)

CHAPTER 4: MENTAL RECREATIONS ABOUT MINECRAFT LOCATIONS

Only at a certain time of day can you see this in the sky over the Overworld. Shortly afterward, it falls, yet it never hits the ground. What is it?

Night.

■

Every biome is a little bit different from the next, with different climates, vegetation, and mobs. But despite all those differences, what will you find in every biome?

The letter "o"—it's in the middle of the word "biome."

■

What cannot be broken, yet can kill you before you know it?

The Void.

■

Where could you go for fun in the sun, except there isn't much sun, so it's not much fun, but it sounds like it could be fun?

The Cold Beach Biome.

You can't be dull here, because this biome is made for you only if you're a fun guy. What is it?

Mushroom Island. (Mushrooms are a kind of fungi.*)*

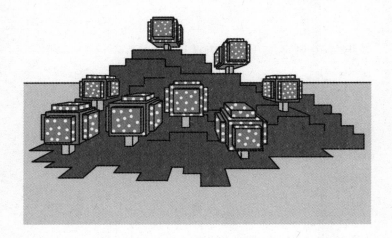

What can run nonstop around the entirety of a house and its yard, yet never move?

A fence.

■

You may be tempted to sleep on me, but I'm not made for that. I'm not without my purpose, protecting you from the Void without moving. What am I?

Bedrock.

■

What's the real overworld of the Overworld?

The End.

I see you, but I will never say hello. But I will probably wave. What am I?

The ocean.

■

What has no legs and no feet but never stops running?

A river.

■

What never gets any wetter, no matter how much it may rain?

The ocean!

■

What's the hardest part about mining in *Minecraft*?

The ground.

■

While my name indicates a conclusion, I come at the beginning . . . of a period of frustration. What am I?

The End.

■

What is water but also solid?

The Swampland Biome.

■

What is above but goes no farther?

The End.

What lines the ocean but otherwise sits nowhere near the water?

Sand.

■

What has a gigantic bed but never stops running long enough to sleep?

A river.

■

What roof in *Minecraft* is always wet, even if it hasn't rained and it's in a dry biome?

The roof of Steve's mouth.

■

Say you're in a room with no windows and no doors, and everything is made of thick rock, except for a wooden table and a bed. How do you get out?

Design and build some exits into it. You're playing Minecraft, *after all.*

■

What time is it here? The same time it was when you went through the gates. What is it?

The Nether.

■

What splits friends from friends and friends from enemies, too?

A fence around a house.

It's got big bones to hold itself up and it swallows human beings whole. Then, when the humans want to go somewhere else, it spits them out alive. What is this thing?

A house.

What can you put in a building that will prevent the Endermen from ever wanting to visit?

Stairs. (Because this hostile mob hates stares.)

■

You're locked inside your house. All you have is a pickaxe. How do you get out?

Unlock the house and walk out!

■

Imagine a biome that's filled with the Vex, and the only tool you can use is a pickaxe. Alex can visit but Steve may not. What's the rule about this world?

Only things with an "X" can be there.

The End is the end, but what comes at the end of the End?

The letter "d."

■

Minecraft programmers and fans alike are trying to figure out what it is that Notch placed between the Overworld and the End. Do you know what it is?

It's the word "and."

■

I'm blue during the day and black at night. I'm full of creatures helpful and mean. What am I?

The sea.

■

You can build ports along bodies of water in Minecraft. Is there a quick way to travel from port to port?

Yes, you can teleport. (But only if you're an Enderman.)

■

A not-so-bright Minecrafter wanted to go to the Taiga, and came to a sign that said "Taiga left." He went to the Jungle instead. Why?

He thought the Taiga had left.

I'm dark and scary and you can sometimes hear me make noise. I'm not a hostile or an item. I'm not a biome but I am a place. So what am I?

A cave.

∎

If Steve and Alex were extremely tired, what biome would they seek out?

The For-rest.

I'm not a mob, item, or player. I live right near the Endermen. What am I?

The End.

∎

What biome doesn't contain any cats, but it sounds like the name of a cat?

Taiga. (It sounds like "tiger.")

What would be the most valuable thing to put in a field in *Minecraft*?

A baseball diamond.

■

***Minecraft* characters don't get sick, but they can catch a cold. How and where?**

If they went to the really cold biomes, they'd certainly get cold.

■

It's invisible and it doesn't weigh anything, but it's certainly something you'll notice on the ground. What is it?

A hole.

Most people try to walk on water, and SPLASH! They fall right into that water. But it can be done in *Minecraft*. What does Steve have to wait for to do that?

He has to make sure the water is in the form of ice or snow.

◼

Look closely at the rain as it comes down from the sky in *Minecraft*. What color is it?

It's watercolor.

◼

How is an old dog like a hill?

While one is a slow pup, the other is a slope up.

What happened to the player who accidentally fell into the Void?

Nothing! He double-tapped space and got out of it just fine.

Stockholm is the capital of Sweden, but it's also right there in *Minecraft*, and it's pretty easy to spot. What does this mean?

Sheep and cows are called livestock. Those livestock are kept on farms, or as you could call one, a "Stock home."

◼

What biome does your house transform into when a creeper walks into it?

The End.

◼

You wake up on a small island. There's no land in sight, you don't have a boat, and there aren't any trees. How do you survive?

Seed a new world.

◼

I'm a field that goes on forever, but I have no grass. You certainly can't walk across me. (You'd perish if you did.) What am I?

The ocean.

◼

Trees grow outdoors, but you might find one in a kitchen inside a *Minecraft* building. In what part of the kitchen would it be?

A: A pan-tree. (Pantry)

You can try to chase me, but you'll never reach me. I'm always way too many miles away, no matter what.

The end of the Far Lands.

■

Even though I don't have eyes, I cry, and I'm always looking over the Overworld. What am I?

The sky. (The crying? That's rain.)

■

Math comes up all the time, but why should you try to avoid doing any math problems in the Jungle Biome?

There are lots of foes there, and no matter what kind of math you do, you might get 8.

■

Say Alex seeded an island in some water. What does that brand-new island have in common with the letter T?

Both the island and the letter come right in the middle of WATER.

■

What would you need to fix a Jack o' Lantern?

A pumpkin patch.

■

What in *Minecraft* can jump higher than a building?

Pretty much anything that moves, because no building in Minecraft *can jump!*

It's at the end of every place, and the end of every biome. You'll find it in a hostile, and in a tamable, and in a neutral, too. What is it?

It's the letter "e."

■

What group of people from Europe would you be most likely to find in the End?

The Finnish.

■

Alex moved all the way across a giant field of grass. It took her hours, but she only moved two feet. What happened in that field?

Alex only has two feet to move – the ones at the end of her legs!

■

In a part of the ocean lived five silverfish and ten squid. But sadly, three of those silverfish and five of the squid died. How many fish stayed in the water?

All of the fish stayed in the water, assuming nobody removed them.

■

Where would the End come before the Overworld?

In a list of Minecraft *places.*

I am unexpected, ferocious, dreadful, violent, chilling, and bad, and when I come I can ruin all your plans. What am I?

A blizzard.

What has wings but stays stuck to the ground (unless a creeper comes along)?

A large building.

■

In which biome will you find me?

Any of them! "Me" comes at the end of "biome."

CHAPTER 5: A BUNCH OF CHALLENGING "MINE" GAMES

Calculating Fun, the *Minecraft* Way

How do you find the answers to these number-based brain twisters about things and places in *Minecraft*? First, think about the clue, then take the number we gave you, enter it into a calculator or a calculator app with old-fashioned numbers…and then turn it upside down.

1. When you build a tower in *Minecraft*, you want it to be:

618

■

2. Another name for the Swampland Biome is a:

608

■

3. Tides flow, but they also:

883

4. Chickens produce these.

5663

5. *Minecraft*'s fish can breathe underwater with the aid of these.

57716

■

6. You don't just like *Minecraft*, you [ANSWER] over it.

553580

■

7. When you dig for ore, you leave these behind.

53704

■

8. You might call your loyal pig this.

604

9. Building things in *Minecraft* is kind of like playing with this real-world toy.

0.637

■

10. Every day, Steve wears blue pants on these.

5637

■

-HSSSS

11. A creeper doesn't talk, but it can certainly do this.

5514

■

12. A witch doesn't so much throw a potion as she does [ANSWER] it.

807

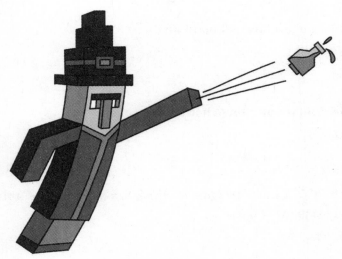

13. This is another name for dirt.

7105

■

14. *Minecraft* isn't a two-player game with two controllers, but rather it's one you play:

0.705

■

15. When you can't figure something out in *Minecraft* or you need tips on how to build something specific, this might be the first place you go.

376006

■

16. When you cut down a tree for wood, it turns into this.

5607

■

17. You use this tool to till dirt.

304

■

18. You'd build these houses in a cold biome.

500761

■

19. The Ender Dragon is *Minecraft*'s version of this video game staple.

5508

Answers:

1. *Big*
2. *Bog*
3. *Ebb*
4. *Eggs*
5. *Gills*
6. *Obsess*
7. *Holes*
8. *Hog*
9. *Lego*
10. *Legs*
11. *Hiss*
12. *Lob*
13. *Soil*
14. *Solo*
15. *Google*
16. *Logs*
17. *Hoe*
18. *Igloos*
19. *Boss*

Amazing *Minecraft* Anagrams

Anagrams are words or phrases you can form by rearranging the letters in another word (or phrase). Can you scramble these words to find the name of a *Minecraft* mob, tool, ore, or biome?

1. DEAL
2. NOT MAID
3. DEER SNOT
4. RED MEAL
5. SLEET
6. CAKE PIX
7. HOVELS
8. GOT IN
9. OPTION
10. ECO LOT
11. SHORE
12. VIRAL GEL
13. REVOKE
14. MOO LINGER
15. ANGER DRONED
16. WRITHE
17. NEW GLOOMS
18. MANNERED
19. HE LURKS
20. EEL KNOTS
21. SLIME
22. ARIEL UNGRADED
23. HOT DIVE
24. SOFTER

25. SPINAL
26. SELFISH MUD ROOMS
27. RESTED
28. I BOLT HOMES
29. MANIC FRET
30. FRANTIC ME

Answers:

1. Lead

2. Diamond

3. Redstone

4. Emerald

5. Steel

6. Pickaxe

7. Shovel

8. Ingot

9. Potion

10. Ocelot

11. Horse

12. Villager

13. Evoker

14. Iron Golem

15. Ender Dragon

16. Wither

17. Snow golem

18. Enderman

19. *Shulker*

20. *Skeleton*

21. *Slime*

22. *Elder Guardian*

23. *The Void*

24. *Forest*

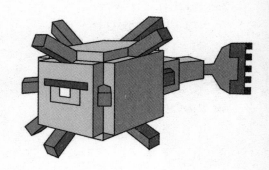

25. *Plains*

26. *Mushroom fields*

27. *Desert*

28. *Hostile mob*

29. *Minecraft*

30. *Minecraft*

Minecraft Spoonerisms

No, this doesn't have anything to do with spoons, so put the stew away. Spoonerisms are a bit of wordplay named after a twentieth-century college professor famous for mixing up the syllables of two different words when he'd say them out loud. We made some *Minecraft* spoonerisms. Can you flip around what needs to be flipped around to get the real *Minecraft* terms?

1. Owe and barrows
2. Runny babbit
3. Hog louse
4. Bay hales
5. Red bock
6. Old gore
7. Wink pool
8. Bake clock
9. Fun slower
10. Pleather ants
11. Dime lye
12. Mone beal
13. Stewing brand
14. Hob mead
15. Habbit ride
16. Tame nag
17. Pingering potion
18. Bungle joat

Answers:

1. *Bow and arrows*

2. *Bunny rabbit*

3. *Log house*

4. *Hay bales*

5. *Bedrock*

6. *Gold ore*

7. *Pink wool*

8. *Cake block*

9. *Sunflower*

10. *Leather pants*

11. *Lime dye*

12. *Bone meal*

13. *Brewing stand*

14. *Mob head*

15. *Rabbit hide*

16. *Name tag*

17. *Lingering potion*

18. *Jungle boat*

Peculiar Pictograms

Look carefully at these arrangements of words to find the answer to each clue. Take in what you see very literally, and say it out loud. That will get you the solutions to these kooky *Minecraft* riddles.

1. If Steve and Alex are out in their boat and Steve falls into the water, he's a
MAN
BOARD

■

2. This is an interesting kind of structure to build, where one floor isn't all the way on top of the lower one.
LE
   VEL

■

3. If you want to build a second entrance into your house, you'd install one of these.
ROOD

■

4. When a creeper explodes a half-finished house, you have to start over on your:
PROGWORKRESS

■

5. It's good to carry a sword, [ANSWER] you come across any hostile mobs.
CAJUSTSE

6. When you get *Minecraft* from the internet, you don't buy it on a CD. Instead, you [ANSWER] it.

L

O

A

D

■

7. Water blocks and rivers are made out of this.

H I J K L M N O

■

8. You'll find these in both wooded and gravelly form.

MOUNTMOUNTMOUNTMOUNTMOUNT
MOUNTMOUNTMOUNTMOUNTMOUNT

■

9. When a hostile mob approaches, do this fast!

HEAD

COVER

COVER

COVER

COVER

■

10. Easily farmed, they're a great food source.

POT OOOOOOOO

Answers:

1. Steve is a "Man over board."

2. Split level

3. Backdoor ("Rood" is "door" backward)

4. Work in progress ("Work" sits in the middle of progress")

5. Just in case ("Just" sits in the middle of "case")

6. Download (It's "load" going downward.)

7. Water (The letters go from "H" to "O," or H2O.)

8. Mountains ("Mount" ten times, or Mount-tens)

9. Head for cover ("Head" + four "cover")

10. Potatoes ("Pot" + 8 "O's")

Antonym Quiz

It's Opposite Day in the Overworld. Can you figure out the *Minecraft* biomes if we tell you their complete and total opposites?

1. Fire Dulls
2. Deforested Valley
3. Complicateds
4. Light Clearing
5. The Beginning
6. Goodskies
7. Upper
8. The Solid

■

Answers:

1. Ice Spikes

2. Wooden Mountains

3. Plains

4. Dark Forest

5. The End

6. Badlands

7. Nether

8. The Void

The *Minecraft* Cockney Rhyming Slang Quiz
There's a tried-and-true method that people in East London, who call themselves cockneys, have long used to talk to each other. It's called cockney rhyming slang: to spice up their conversations, they insert words or phrases that rhyme with the words they mean to say. Can you guess the *Minecraft* terms from their common cockney rhyming slang substitutions?

1. Steve gets energy from eating a "Sistine Chapel."

■

2. Creepers can frighten and blow you up, even without the use of "Chalk Farms."

■

3. To get some light into a structure, you might build in a "Kevin and Linda."

■

4. The first thing you'll notice about a villager is their "Hairy Toes."

■

5. A carrot, potato, or beet is a food you might call an "Uncle Reg."

■

6. Gold blocks are a colored a bright version of "Marti Pellow."

7. If you're lucky you'll nab yourself a "Clothes Peg" from an Ender Dragon.

■

8. Cows can provide plenty of "Lady in Silk."

■

9. A mineshaft is a type of "Drum Roll."

■

10. Steve is almost always wearing his signature blue "Insects and Acts."

■

11. The sounds a ghast makes sound like "Catherine Zeta Jones."

■

12. A meat you can eat is the delicious "Jenson Button."

■

13. When water freezes in the cold it turns into "White Mice."

■

14. This is a lush and exotic biome to find yourself, the "Zippy and Bungle."

■

15. "Habits" can be cute or they can be killer.

16. A skeleton? Not very frightening. It's merely "Sticks and Stones."

■

17. If a creeper blows up a house, he's left a big "Elliot Ness" to clean up.

■

18. When Steve surveys the land to look for places to mine, first he goes for a "Penny's Worth of Chalk."

■

19. What flows in a river? Some "Fisherman's Daughter."

■

20. It's highly recommended you put all your treasure and items in a "Bird's Nest."

Answers

1. Apple

2. Arms

3. Window

4. Nose

5. Veg

6. Yellow

7. Egg

8. Milk

9. Hole

10. Pants

11. Moan

12. Mutton

13. Ice

14. Jungle

15. Rabbits

16. Bones

17. Mess

18. Walk

19. Water

20. Chest

The *Minecraft* Number Code

We've used an "alpha-numeric" code to disguise the names of these *Minecraft* biomes. That means each number corresponds to a different letter of the alphabet. Can you translate the numbers to letters to make some familiar *Minecraft* words? (Here's a hint: M=13.)

1) 19-14-15-23-25 20-21-14-4-18-1

2) 23-15-15-4-5-4 13-15-21-14-20-1-9-14-19

3) 19-20-15-14-5 19-8-15-18-5

4) 20-1-12-12 2-9-18-3-8 6-15-18-5-19-20

5) 10-21-14-7-12-5

6) 13-21-19-8-18-15-15-12 6-9-5-12-4-19

7) 20-8-5 5-14-4

8) 2-1-4-12-1-14-4-19

9) 20-8-5 14-5-20-8-5-18

10) 12-21-11-5-23-1-18-13 15-3-5-1-14

Answers:

1) Snowy Tundra

2) Wooded Mountains

3) Stone Shore

4) Tall Birch Forest

5) Jungle

6) Mushroom fields

7) The End

8) Badlands

9) The Nether

10) Lukewarm Ocean

The *Minecraft* Synonym and Sound-alike Quiz
Can you decipher the clues we've given you below—
synonyms, sound-alike words, and other hints—to figure
out what *Minecraft* items we're talking about?

1. A nickname for a grandma + and object
2. Sleeping place + stone
3. Remaining in place + wet stuff
4. Exits
5. Beach dirt + rocks
6. Corn home + spider home
7. Deceased + bush
8. Happy + king of the jungle
9. A finished book + outside of the mouth
10. De-wrinkler + cube
11. Inflater + family
12. Spirit + beach dirt
13. Making + hard surface
14. To have telephoned + Harry Potter's best friend
15. Cola beverage + 15th letter of the alphabet
16. Bloom + cauldron
17. Leaper
18. 1/4 of a gallon, twice + broken escalator
19. Straw + quit
20. Closest star + bloom
21. Fib + shortage
22. Got up + shrub
23. Tiny green vegetable + 15th letter of the alphabet +
leg joint

24. **Breath + boat operator**

25. **To arrive + to overlook**

26. **Neckwear for businessmen + thing a baby says**

27. **Apple-like fruit + slowly turn foul**

28. **Flying aircraft**

29. **Two doubled + relaxation**

30. **Two-thousand pounds + make art by hand**

31. **Toy baby + fish limb**

Answers

1. Granite (gran + it)

2. Bedrock (bed + rock)

3. Still water (still + water)

4. Leaves (leaves)

5. Sandstone (sand + stone)

6. Cobweb (cob + web)

7. Dead shrub (dead + shrub)

8. Dandelion (dandy + lion)

9. Red tulips (read + two lips)

10. Iron block (iron + block)

11. Pumpkin (pump + kin)

12. Soul sand (soul + sand)

13. Crafting table (crafting + table)

14. Cauldron (called + Ron)

15. Cocoa (Coke + o)

16. Flower pot (flower + pot)

17. *Hopper (leaper)*

18. *Quartz stairs (quarts + stairs)*

19. *Hay bale (hay + bail)*

20. *Sunflower (sun + flower)*

21. *Lilac (lie + lack)*

22. *Rose bush (rose + bush)*

23. *Peony (pea + o + knee)*

24. *Arrow (air + row)*

25. *Compass (come + pass)*

26. *Taiga (tie + "gah!")*

27. *Parrot (pear + rot)*

28. *Plains (planes)*

29. *Forest (four + rest)*

30. *Tundra (ton + draw)*

31. *Dolphin (doll + fin)*

CHAPTER 6: EXTRA TWISTY BRAIN-TWISTERS

What's the capital of the Overworld?

The letter O.

■

What fun pastime includes woods, irons, sand, and lots of holes?

Golf. Did you think we were going to say Minecraft?

Why do players build new buildings in *Minecraft*?

Because the old buildings have already been built.

■

Minecraft players connect from all over the world, but they all ultimately sit in front of a computer and play alone. So where can Steve or Alex find a helping hand?

At the end of their arms.

■

There are so many different versions of *Minecraft*—for computers, consoles, and even smartphones. But no matter which type you play, what's the very first thing in *Minecraft*?

The letter M—it's the very first thing in the word "Mine-craft."

■

Did you hear that Alex hasn't slept in days? She's totally fine, however. Why is that?

She sleeps nights, *not days.*

■

This is the only thing that can destroy bedrock. (And you've probably already heard before that this is true.) What is it?

It's nothing—nothing can destroy bedrock.

Besides all the things made from stone, what do *The Flintstones* **and** *Minecraft* **have in common?**

They both take place upon Bedrock.

■

Steve built a one-story house. There were all kinds of rooms, and a tower, and hundreds of torches. So where did he put the stairs?

He didn't put them anywhere, because a one-story house doesn't need stairs.

■

What tremendous force caused Alex to suddenly stand still, completely frozen in her tracks?

The pause button.

■

What's the best way for Alex to make her bed shorter?

She shouldn't sleep for "long!"

■

What constantly falls on you but never hurts?

The rain.

■

Think of any *Minecraft* **block. It's a cube, so it has 6 surfaces, 8 corners, and 12 edges. Say Steve takes his sword and slices off each corner. How many edges are there now?**

There are 36. The original 12, plus 3 on each of the eight corners, for 24. 12 + 24 = 36.

What begins every game of *Minecraft*?

The word "every" begins the phrase "every game of Mine-craft.*"*

■

What do Steve and his dog have in common?

Pants!

A *Minecraft*er's account got hacked, so he asked for a new password. He received an email from Mojang saying, "Your password is different. I changed it from the old password. Like the old one, it has nine characters." What was the new password?

The password is "different." It has nine letters.

■

Only this can make you invulnerable, powerful, and without limits. And only those enlightened by it can hurt each other. What are they?

A: Cheat codes!

Can you rearrange the letters in "new door" to make one word?

Yes, of course you could. "New door" is an anagram of "one word," meaning they use the same exact letters.

■

However you get there, what will you always find at the very end of *Minecraft*?

The letter "T."

■

Alex makes a gigantic perfect cube of a building consisting of 10 x 10 x 10 cubes, or a total of 1,000 blocks. If she removed one layer of cubes from the outside, how many total cubes would be left?

The remaining cube will be 8 x 8 x 8 cubes, or 512 total blocks. A layer gets taken from every side of the cube, so it would reduce the dimensions by two.

■

What is in the middle of the *Minecraft* sky that you can't see?

The letter "k."

■

What belongs to you but you have to build?

Minecraft. You may own a copy, but you still have to build inside Minecraft to make it worth your while.

Alex is eight years older than Steve. Three years from now, she'll be twice Steve's age. How old are they now?

Alex is 13, and Steve is 5. (They don't look that young!)

■

Can you make a periodic table in *Minecraft*?

Yes. Make a table and just don't use it very often.

■

She's often pregnant when you see her, but she'll never give birth. Who is she?

The moon (when it's full).

■

I don't have feet, or hands, or wings. Still, I churn along as I climb to the sky and beyond. What am I?

Smoke.

■

It's never resting, never still, as it moves silently across the lands. Where it doesn't go, things are way too cool. What is it?

Sunlight.

■

Alex walks into a room where a rabbit is reading a book, a pig is rolling around on its back, and a dolphin is playing cards. Which animal in the room is the smartest?

Alex is, of course.

Steve has six hay bales in front of one of his structures, and then another five hay bales in front of another structure he built. If he moved all those hay bales together and put them in front of that first house, how many hay bales would that make altogether?

Well, if he added six hay bales to five hay bales, he wouldn't have eleven. If he combined them, he'd have one huge hay bale.

You're walking with an empty inventory on a quiet night. You suddenly fall down a hole. From below the hole you wind up in a dungeon and come to three doors. Only one of these can help you escape. The first door leads to a room full of cactus, the second to a horde of zombies, and the third to a deep lake of lava. Which door do you take?

The second door. You were on peaceful mode—it was a quiet night—so no monsters were spawned.

■

You can see me in water, but I never get wet. What am I?

Your reflection.

Of all the hostile mobs, which one has the most money?

Skeletons, because they're literally made up of bones. ("Bones" is a slang term that means money.)

Alex fell into a mineshaft that is twelve feet deep. She could jump three feet, but every time she does, she falls back two feet. How many times would she have to jump to get back onto the surface?

The tenth jump takes her to thirteen feet, and she's out.

■

I move everywhere except the Nether. But once you leave, I'll start moving again. What am I?

Time.

It's an apple involved with *Minecraft*, but it cannot be eaten. What is it?

An Apple iPhone running Minecraft.

■

What appears in two games of *Minecraft* but never in one game of *Minecraft*?

The letter "w." It's in the word "two" but not in "one."

■

It usually rains water in *Minecraft*, but sometimes it rains money. When?

When there's change in the weather.

■

Why don't Minecrafters mind being on Santa's naughty list?

Because they'd find it really lucky if they got free coal.

■

What's the one precious and shiny cube not found in *Minecraft*?

Cubic zirconia.

■

I'm the only thing you can see in the dark, dark night. What am I?

The moon.

What does the average *Minecraft* block have in common with the number 36?

They're both perfect squares.

■

What sickness did Steve get before he constructed a roof?

Shingles.

■

Steve was so cold he stood in the corner of his house. Why?

Because that's where it's 90 degrees.

■

How can something be major when it's minor?

Steve and Alex are major *parts of a game about* miners.

■

The more Steve ventures out in the Far Lands, he leaves more and more of these behind. What are they?

His footsteps.

■

Steve was mining one day, and his pickaxe got caught in his shirt and tore two holes in it. How many holes are in the shirt?

Not two, but six. In addition to the two new ones, it already had four holes: one for each arm, the neck hole, and the bottom.

What belongs to Alex that you use way more than she does?

Her name.

No matter how you choose to play *Minecraft*, this is the last thing Steve does every night.

He goes to sleep.

Think about all the *Minecraft* characters. Now, what has a bottom at its top?

Steve and Alex's legs do.

What's the very first thing that every *Minecraft* player puts in a brand-new structure?

Their player.

What has keys but no locks, has space but no extra room?

The keyboard on the computer you use to play Minecraft.

Steve is in possession of this. It has two legs but cannot walk. What is it?

It's a pair of pants.

■

What has a tongue but can't talk, and gets around without doing any walking itself?

A shoe.

■

What flies, but doesn't have wings, and cries but doesn't have any eyes?

Clouds. They fly through the sky and "cry" raindrops.

■

What fills up a room but doesn't take up any space, and you can walk right through it?

Light.

■

What may change, depending on which biome you're in, but never physically moves?

The temperature.

What is completely dark but made possible by light?

A shadow.

■

Why is the moon the heaviest thing in *Minecraft*?

Because it's full.

■

Can you spawn a lion in *Minecraft*?

Yes, you can spawn a dandelion.

■

Why can't Herobrine clap?

Because he isn't real. If he isn't real, he can't clap!

How can you grow a bird in *Minecraft*?

With bird seed.

■

There are two baby animals permanently attached to Steve at all times. You can't see them, but they're right there with every step. What are they?

Calves. (They're under his pants.)

■

What kind of tree will throw potions at your player?

A tree-o (trio) of witches.

■

This isn't *Fortnite*! No matter what kind of dancing you might try to do in *Minecraft*, it ultimately winds up as this kind of dancing.

Square dancing. (Because everything in Minecraft is square.)

■

I go away every day and come back every night. But unlike some of the creatures around here, I'll never hurt you (or anyone else for that matter). What am I?

The moon.

Every night, this comes around without fail and weakens Steve for hours upon hours. And there's nothing you can do about it. It will always find its way to Steve. What is it?

Sleep.

■

This will kill you, but it isn't a hostile mob. It will happen at some time or another. (But don't worry, you can always just restart the game.) What is it?

Death.

■

In a year's worth of time in *Minecraft*, how many seconds go by?

Just twelve. There's January 2ⁿᵈ, February 2ⁿᵈ, March 2ⁿᵈ...

■

Where would Steve find a hole that's full of sharp weapons . . . but they're stuck to the inside of the hole?

His own mouth. The sharp weapons are his teeth.

■

Try this tongue twister: A zombie zonked out because it needed some zzzzzzz's. How many Z's are in that mouthful?

None. There are no Z's in "that mouthful."

Here's some weird math from *Minecraft* land. Somewhere in the Overworld, 5 + 7 = 12, but 5 + 8 = 1. How, where, and why does this weird math occur?

It's on a clock. 5 + 7 hours = 12 a.m. or 12 p.m. 5 + 8 hours = 1 a.m. or 1 p.m.

■

How is Steve related to his mother's sister's brother-in-law?

That would be Steve's father.

■

Did you know that *Minecraft* has an alphabet? How many letters are in "the Overworld Alphabet?"

It's a trick question. There are literally 20 letters in "the Overworld Alphabet." 3 in "the," 9 in "Overworld," and 8 in "Alphabet." 3 + 9 + 8 = 20.

■

I'm outside *Minecraft*, but if I die your game may completely fall apart. What am I?

Your gaming device's power source.

■

If you make a building in *Minecraft*, how can you make it bigger without tearing it down and starting over or even adding to it?

Simply build another building next to the first one, but make it smaller than the previously existing one. Now the first building is bigger!

What appears only once in *Minecraft*, and probably never appears to an exceptional student?

The letter F.

◾

It lacks a head, but has a neck. It doesn't have hands, but has arms. It's blue and you see it every time you play *Minecraft*. What is it?

It's Steve's shirt, the one he's wearing when you start the game.

◾

It has one entrance and three exits, but it's nothing you can build, and you can't get rid of it, only cover it up. What is it?

It's Steve's shirt, the one he's wearing when you start the game.

◾

If cubism is an art movement in which artists create with little cubes and boxes, who is the most famous and successful cubist of all time?

Notch, because Minecraft *is almost entirely made up of cubes and boxes.*

How many words are in the book you're currently reading right at this moment? (We'll wait while you count.)

There are nine words. They are: "The," "book," "you're," "currently," "reading," "right," "at," "this," and "moment."

■

What passes through sunlight (and torch light, too) and makes its presence felt . . . but never leaves a shadow?

The wind.

■

A chicken somehow goes soaring across the sky in the Jungle Biome only to fall into a mine cart and speed off to the Gravelly Mountains. Where in the Overworld did that chicken come from?

An egg.

■

In this sentence, one word is spelled incorrectly. Can you figure out which word it is? Look closely.

The word that's spelled incorrectly is . . . incorrectly. (Which we spelled correctly!)

■

What can you cover something with that actually makes it stand out more?

Light!

Before he created *Minecraft*, what was the name of the guy who created *Minecraft*?

It was the same as it is now: Magnus Persson.

■

Alex once built a structure at eye level. What's unique about eye level?

Both "eye" and "level" are palindromes, meaning they read the same forward and backward.

■

Without the use of any special mods, how could you play baseball in *Minecraft*?

With the bats and a diamond.

■

What's the quickest and most effective way to create a waterfall in *Minecraft*?

First, fill up a bucket of water. Then knock it over.

■

So why don't we have a brain twister on this page about Steve's bed?

It hasn't been made up yet.

■

Steve wears two caps everywhere he goes, yet his head is always bare. What's going on?

He has two kneecaps.

Steve and Alex are adults, but how are they like children or teens?

Because they're miners (minors).

■

You don't need them to hold things together, but there are nails in *Minecraft*. Where can you find them?

On the fingers of Alex, Steve, and the villagers.

■

Alex once had a boat. What is its name?

"What" is its name.

■

Steve is trapped in his house with a swarm of bats. What should he do?

Open the door to let the bats out!

■

Which kind of *Minecraft* game can you never win but also never lose?

A game of Minecraft *you never play.*

■

Can you telephone from *Minecraft*?

Yes, a phone is a small brick in your pocket and Minecraft is a video game. So you can certainly "tell a phone from Minecraft."

Where would be the one place Steve would most hate for you to put his chest?

Right on top of Steve.

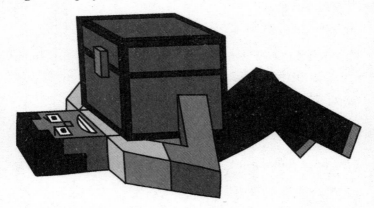

Alex rested a ladder against the side of the five-story house she'd just built. While on it one day, she fell off . . . but it's okay, because she didn't get hurt. How is that possible?

Alex was standing on the bottom rung of the ladder . . . and she fell about three inches.

There aren't a lot of keys in *Minecraft*, but what's the best key you can get?

Luck-key (lucky).

Of all the things in *Minecraft*, this is the one thing that, curiously, Steve can hold in his right hand, but not his left hand. What is it?

It's his left elbow.

When is Alex not herself?

When she's running from a hostile mob and suddenly turns . . . into her house.

■

If you know it, it ceases to exist, but it continues to be if you don't know it. What is it?

A brain twister!

CHAPTER 7: RIDDLES FROM THE VILLAGE

A farmer in the village has 16 sheep. All but seven die. How many are left?

Seven. The other ones die.

■

A farmer over in the village has five chickens and two horses, and he lives with his wife. How many feet are on that farm?

Just four. His wife has two feet, he has two feet, chickens don't have feet (just talons), and each horse has four hooves apiece.

■

Say it took eight villagers a total of ten hours to build a wall around the village. How long would it take four villagers to build it?

A: No time at all. The wall is already built, so it doesn't need to get constructed.

■

Steve tried to lift all of his collected treasures, but he hurt himself. He went to a doctor in the village, who gave him a diagnosis. What did the doctor say was Steve's issue?

Chest pains.

While most villagers mean no harm to you, this villager isn't that kind of villager. Who is it?

It's an illager.

A villager has nine children. Half of them are girls. How is this possible?

Not only is one half girls, the other half is, too—all nine kids are girls.

What do a cave full of zombies and the village butcher shop have in common?

Both are full of dead meat.

A man in the village has married dozens of the village's women. He himself has never been married. How is this possible?

He's the village minister.

A villager arrived in a new village on Friday, stayed three days, then left on Friday. How did he come and go on Friday if he only stayed for three days?

He came and went on a horse—a horse named Friday.

What's hard to find, easy to lose, worth more than gold, and doesn't cost anything?

Friendship!

Why would the village barber rather cut the hair of two brown-haired villagers than one yellow-haired villager?

They would get paid more for two haircuts, rather than just one.

Who are the most patient people in the village?

Doctors—they see patients every day.

There's a baker in the village who's best known for making nothing. So what does he *do* all day?

He bakes doughnuts . . . which have a big hole in the middle.

■

If a villager is carrying torches but drops one, what does he become?

A torch lighter.

■

There's a villager in the village who makes bridges out of silver and fills in holes with gold and metal ore. But she never leaves the village. Who is this?

She's the village dentist. (The holes she fills with gold and metal are cavities.)

There's a villager in the village who shaves twenty times a day. Yet when he goes home in the evening, he still has a thick beard. What's his deal?

He's the village barber.

There's a villager named Oliver who is six feet tall, works in the village butcher shop, and wears size 11 shoes. What does he weigh?

Meat. He works in the butcher shop.

There's a villager named Oliver who is six feet tall, works in the village butcher shop, and wears size 11 shoes. What does he weigh?

■

The village's math teacher asked her top student a tricky problem: "Divide 50 by half, and add 20." The student got it right. What was her response?

120. It's tricky because you're not supposed to split 50 in half; you're supposed to divide it by half. 50 divided by ½ = 100. Add 20, and it's 120.

Villagers have long noses. Why can't a villager's nose be 12 inches long?

Because then it would be a foot.

■

How many square feet are in the village?

It depends on how many villagers (with their square feet) are standing around in the village at the time.

■

Mr. Villager and Mrs. Villager were walking home from the market with their groceries when Mr. Villager began to complain that his load was too heavy. Mrs. Villager said, "I don't know what you're complaining about. If you made me carry just one of your parcels, I would have twice as many as you. And if I gave you just one of mine, we would have equal loads." How many parcels was each carrying?

Mrs. Villager was carrying seven parcels, while Mr. Villager was carrying five.

■

How can a villager hold a piece of string with one end in each hand, and tie a knot in the string without letting go of either end?

They should cross their arms before they grab each end of the string. Once they uncross their arms, the string will tie into a knot.

Steve thinks he might have a cavity. When should he seek out a dentist in the village?

At tooth-hurty.

Alex has a bucket containing six apples. How does she divide them among six hungry villager kids so each one gets an apple, but one apple stays in the bucket?

She hands each of the first five kids an apple. Then the sixth kid gets an apple . . . that stays at the bottom of the bucket.

Over in the village, two girls were born to the same mother, on the same day, at the same time, in the same month and year. Yet these baby girls are not twins. What gives?

The two babies are two out of three triplets.

A villager told another villager about his children. "All are tall but two. All are short but two, and all are medium but two." How many children did he have in all?

He has three children altogether.

A villager places a twenty-foot tether on her hose, but the horse sees there's food about forty feet away. How can the horse get to that food?

The horse can just go for it. The other end of the tether isn't connected to anything.

A villager walks to the village market. On the way he says hello to three grandmas, two mailmen, a farmer, two doctors, a horse keeper, and three little kids. How many people were walking to the market?

Just the one villager.

◾

A villager has as many brothers as she does sisters. But her brothers only have half a brother for every sister. How many brothers and sisters are there in the family?

There are a total of four sisters and three brothers.

◾

Steve sees a boat full of villagers. But there isn't a single person on board. How can this be?

The villagers aren't single – they're all married people.

◾

Three villagers head out to the river with their fishing rods to catch some dinner. If the three of them catch three fish in three minutes, then how many villagers would it take to catch one thousand fish in one thousand minutes?

Just those same three villagers. They're already catching fish at a rate of one per person per minute, so in one thousand minutes those three people would grab one thousand fish.

Hamm lives on a little farm outside the village with four dogs. Their names are Hank, Babe, Willie, and Barry. There's a fifth dog, too. What's that dog named?

Hamm is the fifth dog.

If a villager charges you, what should you do?

You should pay them what you owe them.

What do you call a villager who doesn't have all his fingers on one hand?

That's any *villager, seeing as how nobody has* all *of their fingers on just one hand.*

Three villagers, Moody, Toody, and Poody, all have different jobs in the village as either a doctor, a teacher, and a policeman. If Moody hates blood, and neither she nor Poody likes kids, what is everyone's job?

Moody would have to be the policeman, as her dislike of blood and children means she can't be the doctor or the teacher. Poody doesn't like kids, so he isn't the teacher either. And since Moody is the police officer, Poody is the doctor. That makes Toody the teacher.

■

Four villagers are at home in their cottage. The father villager prepares dinner while the mother villager works in the garden. One of their two kids is in the basement playing a board game. What's the other kid villager doing?

Playing the board game with the other villager kid.

■

Some villagers held a big party and hired a magician to entertain the little kids. While standing in front of a tub full of water, he told the children he'd give an emerald to the party guest who could keep his or her head underwater for more than five minutes. Just one kid took the magician up on the offer, and won his emerald. He didn't even get his hair wet. How'd he do it?

He put a bottle of water on top of his head. And then he stayed under water, literally, for those five minutes.

A villager has a son who is one-fifth of his age. After 21 years, he'll be double that age. The villager's wife is seven times older than their daughter, and she'll be three times as old as the daughter in eight years. How old are the little villagers right now?

The son is seven, and the daughter is four.

■

There are so many dangers in the Overworld that it makes life quite difficult. How many birthdays will the average villager enjoy in their lifetime?

Just one. Villagers, like you, have just one birthday—the day they're born. All other days you call your birthday are really just the anniversary of your true birthday.

Two fathers from the village and their two sons go out fishing. Everybody catches exactly one fish, but their total haul is only three fish. How is this possible?

There are three people: a grandfather, a father and his son. The grandfather is one of the two fathers, and the father is both a father and a son.

■

There are a lot of people in the small village, but by and large they don't seem to be very smart. Why is this?

The population is dense.

■

One day a villager fell. She stayed unconscious for about eight hours, but when she came to, she wasn't the least bit hurt. What happened to the villager?

She fell, all right...she fell asleep.

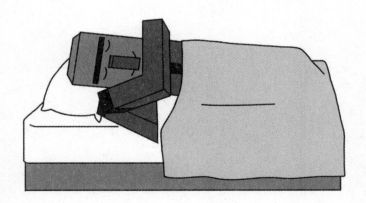